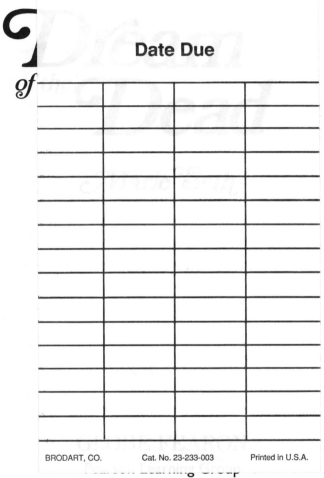

**Date Due**

| | | | |
|---|---|---|---|
| | | | |
| | | | |
| | | | |
| | | | |
| | | | |
| | | | |
| | | | |
| | | | |
| | | | |
| | | | |
| | | | |
| | | | |
| | | | |
| | | | |
| | | | |
| | | | |
| | | | |

# The PACEMAKER BESTELLERS

## Bestellers I

Diamonds in the Dirt
Night of the Kachina
The Verlaine Crossing
Silvabamba
The Money Game

Flight to Fear
The Time Trap
The Candy Man
Three Mile House
Dream of the Dead

## Bestellers II

Black Beach
Crash Dive
Wind Over Stonehenge
Gypsy
Escape from Tomorrow

The Demeter Star
North to Oak Island
So Wild a Dream
Wet Fire
Tiger, Lion, Hawk

## Bestellers III

Star Gold
Bad Moon
Jungle Jenny
Secret Spy
Little Big Top

The Animals
Counterfeit!
Night of Fire and Blood
Village of Vampires
I Died Here

## Bestellers IV

Dares
Welcome to Skull Canyon
Blackbeard's Medal
Time's Reach
Trouble at Catskill Creek

The Cardiff Hill Mystery
Tomorrow's Child
Hong Kong Heat
Follow the Whales
A Changed Man

Series Director: Tom Belina

Designer: Richard Kharibian

Cover and Illustrations: Jim McConnell

ISBN 0-8224-5256-1
Printed in the United States of America

**8  9  10  11  1      05  04  03  02**

Globe Fearon
Pearson Learning Group

**1-800-321-3106**
**www.pearsonlearning.com**

# CONTENTS

CHAPTER **1**

## THE POND

"Ghosts!" Diana Fessler said. "Do you have real ghosts here?"

"Now wait a minute!" Andrew Lang said, laughing. "Jenny, tell your friend you were joking. Don't frighten her as soon as she begins her visit."

Jenny Lang smiled. "All right, Uncle Andrew. Diana, I was joking. But this is the kind of big old house that *should* have a ghost. And there *are* strange noises. A lot of strange things happened when we first moved in."

"It was all in your mind," Andrew Lang said. "After we talked it over, they stopped, didn't they?"

"Yes, and I was glad," Jenny said. "I was really frightened for a while. But people around here believe in the ghost. Even Mark does, I think. And he is a parson's son."

Mark Woodburn smiled. He was tall and good-looking. "No, Jenny," he said. "I don't believe in ghosts. But I *have* seen things here that I can't explain. And I told your uncle when you came that no one stays here long. That's all I said."

"No more talk of ghosts now while we eat," Mr. Lang said. "Diana, I can't tell you how glad I am that you came to Scotland for the summer. It is good for Jenny to have company here."

"Yes," Jenny said, "Mark and his father, the parson, are our only neighbors. It's nice to have company. For all of us."

"I was so glad when you sent me the ticket," Diana said. "I still can't believe I'm in Scotland."

Diana was an old friend of Jenny's. She used to spend her summer vacations with Jenny and her uncle, Andrew Lang.

"I'm glad you could come," Jenny said. "It will be just like the old days when you used to stay at our house for the summer. Remember those long walks we used to take?"

"I remember how Diana used to walk in her sleep," Mr. Lang said. "We were afraid she would walk right out the door. Do you still walk in your sleep, Diana?"

"Oh, no," Diana answered. "I haven't walked in my sleep for a long time."

"That's good," said Mark. "We wouldn't want you walking off and getting lost. There are very few houses around here for miles. Just this house, our house, and the church."

"It is rather out-of-the-way," Diana said. "How did you happen to come here?" she asked Mr. Lang.

"My people were from around here," he said. "Long, long ago, of course. This summer my wife wanted a long visit with her sisters. I decided to come here—to this part of Scotland. I have always wanted to. Jenny came to keep an eye on me. This was the only house we could rent. So here we are."

Diana looked about the room. Everything she could see was large and old. It was hard to see much by the light of the candles. The house had no electricity. It was too far out of the way for electricity.

There were two pictures on the wall across from her.

Diana went over to look at them.

One was of a man in an army coat and hat. The kind they wore long ago. He looked mean, Diana decided.

The other picture was of a young woman. Diana wondered who she was. She couldn't see the picture clearly by the light of the candles.

"Her name was Elizabeth Angus," Mark said, as if reading her mind. "She was the daughter of the man who built this house, over two hundred years ago."

He turned to Mr. Lang. "You should take that picture down."

"It isn't our house, Mark. We must leave things as they are," Mr. Lang said. "Besides, what trouble can a picture cause?"

Mark didn't answer.

There was a flash of lightning outside. Diana jumped and then felt silly.

Mark gave her a warm smile. "That's just one of our sudden storms," he told her. "I think I'd better be going before the rain begins."

"Yes," Mr. Lang said. "I wouldn't want you to get lost in a storm and walk into the bog."

Mark said to Diana, "I don't know if you know about bogs. They are fields of mud. Deep, deep mud. You sink down and down and are never seen again. I don't want to frighten you. But a bog is something to keep away from. There is one near the graveyard next to the church."

"I'll remember," Diana said.

After he left, Diana said, "How nice he is, Jenny."

"He was brought up well," Mr. Lang said.

"But he is still nice," Jenny said, laughing.

Diana could feel her eyes getting heavy.

"You have had a long trip, Diana," Mr. Lang said. "Jenny, why don't you take her up to her room now."

"Take a candle," Jenny said. "We always have to remember to carry a candle at night."

Diana said, "It's going to be hard getting used to not having electricity."

They went up the long turning stairs and down a long dark hall. They turned into another hall and went into the last room.

"We don't use most of the rooms," Jenny said. "You will get lost at first. But your room is right next to mine. Uncle Andrew is just at the other end of the hall."

Diana said, "Oh, Jenny, it will be so good to have our long talks again."

"Let's talk tomorrow," Jenny said. "I'll let you sleep now."

There was an oil lamp on a small table. She showed Diana how to light it.

Jenny left the room. Diana went to the window. But she couldn't see anything. She could only hear the rain and the wind.

She looked around the room. Next to the lamp was a large old music box. Diana picked it up. The key would not turn. It was broken. She put it back on the table and got ready for bed.

With the noise of the storm outside, she didn't think she would fall asleep soon. But she did. She dreamed about her long trip over the ocean.

Her dream was not the way her real trip had been. In her dream the airplane was not flying in good weather. There was a storm. The plane shook as lightning hit it again and again.

Just as the plane was about to crash, a voice screamed. It said, "Help me! Please help me!"

Diana sat up in bed, shaking.

"What a dream!" she said. "I'm glad it's over. It was so real!"

But there it was again. Above the noise of the wind she thought she heard someone scream, "Help me! Please help me!"

Diana ran to the window. She opened it, letting in the rain.

"Where are you? I'll help you. Tell me where you are," she shouted.

In a flash of lightning she could make out a pond. Near the edge of the pond, she could see someone splashing in the water.

There was another flash of lightning. Now she could not see anyone in the pond. Even with the wind blowing, the water was still. There were no waves at the edge.

There was no time now to think how strange that was.

CHAPTER **2**

## THE GIRL IN THE GRAVEYARD

"Diana, what is it? I heard you shouting," Jenny said. She ran into the room with a candle.

"Someone out there needs help. Someone in the pond," said Diana. She rushed to the door.

"Wait, Diana," Jenny said. "What do you mean? What pond? Who needs help?"

"I'll tell you on the way," Diana said. She ran down the hall. "Help me find the stairs."

Jenny ran beside her. She pointed out the way. As they ran, the candle went out.

"Stop, Diana. We can't run down the stairs in the dark. Wait until I light this candle again," Jenny said. "Tell me what happened."

"I heard a woman scream for help. In a flash of lightning, I saw her in the pond. The next time the lightning flashed she was gone," Diana said.

"But, Diana, *there is no pond*," Jenny said.

They looked at each other in the low light of the candle.

"I saw a pond," Diana said. "I saw it very clearly."

Jenny asked, "Are you sure you heard someone scream? Could you have dreamed it? Or could it have been the wind?"

"Well, I *was* having a bad dream," Diana said. "Only I heard it again after I woke up. I couldn't hear it too clearly because of the sound of the wind."

"There you are then," Jenny said. "Listen, Diana, this house does strange things to people. Mark and his father won't tell me much. But I heard Mark tell Uncle Andrew that strange things have happened here before."

Diana and Jenny walked back down the hall.

"Yes, you said you had trouble when you first came here," Diana said. "What kind of trouble? Can you tell me?"

"I heard things, too," Jenny said. "Or I thought I did. And I thought I saw things sometimes. I was never really sure. Then one day I was all by myself in the house. It was a hot day. Suddenly I was so cold. As cold as ice. I just shook from the cold."

They went into Diana's room. Diana sat down on the bed. Jenny sat in a large soft chair.

"What did you do?" Diana asked.

"I ran out and looked for Uncle Andrew," Jenny said. "We had a long talk. He said I was probably coming down with a cold. Or I had been standing by an open window. I told him about the other things."

"Was he surprised? Or did he just laugh?" Diana said.

Jenny said, "Uncle Andrew told me it's like that in some old houses. No one knows why. He told me what to do the next time something strange happened. He said just to tell myself over and over that it wasn't real. And it worked."

"You don't see or hear strange things now?" asked Diana.

Jenny smiled. "Sometimes I almost do. But right away I tell myself it isn't happening. It stops and it doesn't frighten me any more." She stood up. "We had better get to sleep now."

"Good night, Jenny," Diana said as her friend left the room.

It was some time before Diana could get back to sleep. She turned from side to side. Now and then she thought she heard a voice calling far away. Calling her name.

"It's only the wind. It's only the wind," she told herself over and over.

She had a strange empty feeling. She felt she had let down someone who needed her help.

"I want to help you," she whispered. "But I don't know how." Hearing the words made her feel silly. She smiled and went to sleep.

In the morning the first thing she did was look out the window.

She saw green grass, a garden, and trees. There was no pond in sight. There was just a clear space in the middle of a circle of big trees. She could also see the old church and the graveyard next to it.

It was a cool, gray morning so she put on a pretty yellow dress.

Jenny's room was empty. Diana found her way down to the kitchen.

"Jenny, where did you learn to cook with a wood stove?" she said, laughing.

"Mark showed me how," Jenny said. "Poor Uncle Andrew ate a lot of burned food at first. But now I have the hang of it. Mark and his father do their own cooking."

Diana said, "Then the parson's wife—"

"Parson Woodburn was never married," Jenny said to her friend. She saw the puzzled look on Diana's face.

Jenny explained, "Mark's parents died when he was five or six. The parson took him in. Mark doesn't talk much about it. But I know he looks on Parson Woodburn as a father. Mark took Woodburn for his last name. He did it because he wanted to."

"Oh," Diana said. "Then both of you lost your parents when you were little. That must make you even better friends."

"Don't get the wrong idea about Mark and me," Jenny told Diana, with a smile. "We are just friends. Nothing more."

Just then they heard Andrew Lang coming down the stairs. He was singing a happy song. He went out the side door.

"He is so happy here," Jenny said. "I'm so glad we came to Scotland. Oh, look, I haven't set the table yet."

"I'll do that," Diana said. She flew about finding dishes and cups.

Hearing that Jenny wasn't interested in Mark made her feel like singing. But that was silly. She had only met him once.

Mr. Lang came in with some eggs.

Diana ate a big breakfast. At home she was never hungry in the morning.

After breakfast Mr. Lang went to the study to read his mail. Jenny and Diana heated water to wash the dishes.

The sun came out. Light streamed in the windows. The bad dream and strange feelings of last night seemed far away.

Later Mr. Lang took Diana to see the garden.

Diana couldn't stop thinking about Mark Woodburn. From time to time she looked toward the church.

Then she saw someone walking in the graveyard. It could be Mark. He was too far away for her to be sure.

A woman was standing in the man's path. She was wearing a long white dress. The man walked right by her without slowing down.

"Take a look at this row of greens," Mr. Lang said. "Did you know that you can cut them and they will grow right back?"

"No, I didn't," Diana said. When she looked up again, the man was much closer. The woman was gone.

"Here comes Mark," Mr. Lang said. "I'm going in for a basket. I want to cut some greens for lunch."

Mark Woodburn gave Diana a warm smile and said hello.

She smiled back and said, "Who was the woman in the graveyard? Does she live around here?"

Mark's smile was gone. "What woman?" he said. "What are you talking about?"

"The woman in the long dress," Diana said. "I wonder why she is wearing a long dress on such a warm day."

Mark gave her an angry look. "There was no woman there, Diana. The sun was playing tricks with your eyes."

"But she was right in your path," Diana said. "You almost bumped into her. You must have seen her."

Mark looked so angry that Diana was afraid. "I tell you that there was no woman in the graveyard!" he shouted.

CHAPTER **3**

## THE FACE IN THE MIRROR

Diana looked at Mark with wonder. She didn't know what to say.

"You should not have come," Mark said in a cold voice. "All of you should have stayed away. Why wouldn't Mr. Lang listen to me?"

He walked toward the house with quick steps. Diana followed slowly.

Why was Mark so angry with her? What had she said? Did the woman in the graveyard mean something to him? Something he did not want her to know about?

She didn't see him in the house. She heard voices from the study. But she couldn't make out the words.

Diana headed for the kitchen to look for Jenny.

In the hall she saw a mirror. She stopped to see what the wind had done to her hair.

The hall was dark. The mirror was old. The only light came from the room across the hall.

But in the mirror she could see a tear on her face.

"Mark made me cry. I didn't even know it," she said to herself. She rubbed her face. The tear was still there.

"How strange!" she said. Her heart began to beat fast.

Suddenly she saw that the face in the mirror had very long hair. Not short, like hers. And a different color—light brown. Her own hair was dark brown.

Diana began to shake. She backed away from the mirror, her heart pounding.

She looked behind her to see if there was someone there. No one was there. But across the hall she saw the picture of Elizabeth Angus.

"Of course," Diana said. "That's what I saw in the mirror. The girl in the picture. That has to be it."

Diana looked closer at the picture. The girl did look very sad. She was not crying, however.

Light from the window was shining on something in the picture. It was something the girl was wearing around her neck. It looked like a gold locket.

"Maybe that locket was the tear I saw," Diana said to herself. "Maybe it was a trick of the light."

Behind the girl in the picture was a circle of young trees. The trees were around a small round pond.

Her heart began to beat fast again.

The pond looked just like the one in her dream. It was the same pond.

She jumped when she heard a voice behind her. It was Mark.

"I'm so sorry for the way I spoke to you," Mark said. "There was no call for it."

"But why were you so angry?" Diana asked. "I don't understand."

Mark said, "I can't explain. It would only frighten you. How I hate this house! I said you shouldn't have come here, Diana."

Jenny called out from the kitchen, "Mark, is that you? The stove is too hot again. Come and tell me how to fix it."

Mark fixed the stove and then left. He said he would try to come back after dinner.

After he left, Jenny said, "He checks up on us every day." She laughed. "It is almost as if he thinks there will be trouble."

The day went fast. The sun stayed out.

Jenny and Diana took a long walk in the afternoon. They walked in a big circle around the house.

When they were in the graveyard, Jenny pointed to the left. "Don't ever walk too far over that way," she said.

"Why not?" asked Diana. "What is over there?" She could see that there was a lot of tall grass but not many trees.

"The bog," Jenny said.

"Did anyone ever get caught in it?"

Jenny said, "Mark says long, long ago a girl was lost. It was the little sister of the girl in that picture in the house. She was never found. They decided she went down in the bog."

Suddenly Diana went cold. It felt like someone had put ice down her back.

"You're shaking. What is wrong?" Jenny said.

"I don't know. I'm cold," said Diana.

"It's this graveyard," Jenny said. "These big old trees keep out the sun. Let's go."

Diana felt better when they were back in the house. She helped Jenny fix dinner.

Diana said, "Did Mark tell you he hates this house?"

"He told you that?" Jenny said. "But then why does he come every day?"

"He comes to see the people, not the house," Diana pointed out.

"It is strange," Jenny said. "He seems to worry about us so much. I don't know what he thinks is going to happen."

Mark came over after dinner. The four of them played cards. It was late when Mark left.

After he left, Mr. Lang said, "Jenny, did you see what I saw?"

"See what?" Diana asked.

Mr. Lang and Jenny laughed.

"You and Mark," Jenny said. "His eyes never light up when he looks at me. But they did the first time he saw you. There is an electricity between the two of you."

Mr. Lang said, "Someone might think that you and Mark were old friends."

Diana could feel her face burn. "I don't know what you mean," she said. But she did know. She had felt it, too.

She went up to her room. For a long time she stood by the window. She looked up at the stars. She wondered how Mark felt.

Then she went to bed. Right away she began to dream. She knew it was a dream.

In her dream she got up. She walked down the hall in the dark. She went down the stairs and out the door.

"I have to find it," she said.

Diana walked to the edge of the pond.

"It fell here by the edge," she said out loud. "I saw it fall by this tree. But why are the trees so large? So large and old?"

She got down on the ground. Her fingers dug into the earth.

"Diana, what in the world are you doing?"

Diana looked up. Jenny was standing over her. They were outside.

There was a full moon. Diana looked around. She could see her fingers were black with dirt. They hurt from digging.

She looked for the pond.

There was no pond. She knew there was no pond. Why couldn't she get it out of her mind?

CHAPTER **4**

## THE TOMBSTONE

"Diana, I'm sorry. I know I should not wake
you when you walk in your sleep. But what are
you doing?" Jenny said.

"I have to find it," Diana said. She was still
half in her dream.

"Find what?" Jenny asked as she helped her
up. "What are you looking for?"

"I don't know," Diana said. "I had to find
something. I knew it was right here. Right here
near this tree."

"Why can't you dream in bed like other
people?" Jenny said. She smiled at her friend.

"I haven't walked in my sleep for years,"
Diana said. "I thought I was over that."

"You frightened me," Jenny said. "I was still
awake. I heard you go past my door. I saw that
you didn't have a light. So I went after you with
a candle."

They went back inside. Jenny walked with Diana to her door.

"Do you want me to lock you in?" Jenny asked.

Diana said, "No, I'll put a chair in front of the door. Remember when I used to have to do that every night?"

Diana lay awake for a long time. Too many strange things were happening.

Diana was afraid.

"Is there something wrong with me?" she wondered.

At last she went to sleep. There were no more dreams that night.

At breakfast Mr. Lang told her she did not look well.

"I'm all right. I didn't sleep well," she said.

She wished she could tell him about her fears. But he would just tell her not to think about it. Or maybe he would think the kind thing to do would be to send her home. She didn't want to go home, away from Jenny. Away from Mark.

Even Jenny didn't know all of it. She didn't know about the face in the mirror. For some reason, Diana didn't want to tell her about it. Not yet. She couldn't make up her own mind about it.

After breakfast Mark came over. He was riding a horse. He was leading two other horses.

"Hello, Diana. Hello, Jenny," he said. "Would you like to go riding? I brought some horses over for you."

"I would love to," Jenny said. "But I have to write a letter now. You two go."

"Mr Lang, would you like to ride this morning?" Mark asked.

"Not this morning," Mr. Lang said. "I have some work to do."

Diana knew that Jenny and Mr. Lang were being kind. They were letting her and Mark have some time together.

She wondered if Mark knew it. It was hard to tell what Mark was thinking.

Diana told Mark she had never been on a horse. Mark showed her how to get on.

She looked down. It seemed a long way to the ground.

Mark laughed. "That horse is so old it can hardly walk. Don't you worry. If you want to stop, just pull. But don't pull too hard or fast."

They rode for half an hour.

Mark said, "You are doing great for your first ride, Diana. But I think we should rest. Here is a good spot."

Diana enjoyed riding. But it felt good to get off the horse for a while.

They sat down on a large rock.

There were so many things Diana wanted to know about Mark. Yet she felt she knew him without knowing about his past.

"Were you born near here?" she asked.

"Yes," he answered. He didn't say any more for a minute. Then he added, "I was born in the house you are staying in."

"Oh," Diana said.

Mark was looking down in an angry way.

"I know you don't like to talk about the house," Diana said. "But can I ask you about that picture of the girl?"

"What about it?" Mark said. He was looking away from her.

"Who was the girl in the picture? Do you know anything about her?" Diana asked.

Mark's voice was hard. But he looked sad, not angry.

"She killed herself," he said. "She drowned herself."

Diana jumped to her feet. "I don't believe you!" she shouted.

"What do you mean?" Mark said. "Why would I make it up?"

"Oh, Mark, what a silly thing for me to say!" Diana said. "I don't even know why I said it. I didn't know I was going to say it."

"Let's get back on our horses," Mark said. "I want to show you something." He smiled at her. But his eyes were full of worry.

They rode to the graveyard. At the edge of it he pointed out a tombstone. They got off their horses.

"The writing on it is very old," he said. "It's hard to read. See if you can make it out."

It took Diana a long time. Mark didn't help her. Diana knew he wanted her to read it for herself.

She said, "The name on top is Elizabeth Angus. The stone says she died in 1778. That's two hundred years ago."

"See if you can make out the other words," Mark said.

Little by little, Diana read:

*"Cut short her own life at the start.*

*Drowned because of a broken heart."*

They didn't speak for a while.

After a few minutes Diana said, "I saw a pond in that picture of her. Did she drown in that pond?"

"Yes," Mark said.

"Mark, it all happened so long ago. Two hundred years ago. Why does it hurt you to talk about it?" Diana said.

Mark looked at her. "The pond was near the house. It was inside that circle of trees."

"But there is no pond there," Diana said.

"Not any more," Mark said. "The pond was filled in after my parents drowned in it."

CHAPTER **5**

## THE STORY OF ELIZABETH

"I didn't want to tell you, Diana," Mark said. "I didn't want to frighten you."

"Sometimes it's worse not to know something," Diana said. "There is too much going on that I don't understand. I am not a child that you should keep things from me."

"I have to start way back," Mark said. "Long before what happened to my parents."

"All right," Diana said. They sat down again to talk.

"There is a lot that I don't understand either," Mark said. "My father—the parson, that is—won't talk about it."

"How did you learn what you do know?" Diana asked.

"From friends and neighbors," Mark said. "There was a kind old woman who used to cook and clean for us. She helped the parson bring me up. She liked to talk about the old days."

"Does it begin with Elizabeth Angus?" Diana asked the parson's son.

"Yes," Mark said. "Elizabeth Angus was very young. She was in love with a man named Ian Mackenzie. Her father didn't like it."

"Because she was too young?" Diana asked.

"That was part of it," Mark said. "Also, the Mackenzies were poor. They had a small farm. Ian was in the army. So was Elizabeth's father. Of course, he was much higher up than Ian."

"That sounds bad for Ian," Diana said.

"It was," Mark said. "Elizabeth's father had him sent far away. To some war or other. I don't know just when this happened. Elizabeth's father may have hoped that he would be killed. Or that Elizabeth would forget about him."

"What happened?" Diana asked.

"Some people say that news came that Ian was dead. And Elizabeth went out that night and drowned herself."

Diana said, "Why is it that I know that can't be true?"

Mark said, "Other people told me that Elizabeth would not believe Ian was dead. Her father told her and she would not believe him."

"Then why would she drown herself?" Diana said. "For what reason?"

"I don't know," Mark said. "Some people even say that the news of Ian's death came after Elizabeth had drowned. How ever it happened, that was the beginning of the end of the Angus family. Elizabeth's little sister died in the bog a month later. Her parents died soon after. The house was left to other members of the family. They stayed for only a few weeks. The house was rented several times. No one stayed long. After that it was empty for many, many years."

"You mean people were afraid to stay in it?" Diana said.

"I guess so," Mark said. "At last the Angus family died out. The house and land were sold. The new owners moved in. They left the next morning with food still on the table."

"The house was empty again," Diana said.

"For a few years," Mark said. "Then my father wanted to get married. But he had no money. He was a painter. So he and my mother said they would look after the house and grounds. They moved in as soon as they were married."

"And they stayed," Diana said.

"One night when I was six I heard my mother scream outside. I ran out. My mother was in the pond. She was caught in the weeds."

"You still remember all of it, don't you?" Diana said.

"Like the night it happened," said Mark. His hands were shaking. "My father jumped in to save her. He told me to run for help. I ran to the parson."

"And came back to find them both drowned. Poor Mark," Diana said. "But did it have something to do with Elizabeth Angus?"

Mark said, "I don't see how it could. But other people believe it did. I just know I hate the house. Too many bad things happen there."

"Did you tell Mr. Lang about all this?" asked Diana.

"I told him some of it. He laughed at the idea that something could be wrong with the house."

"Mark, I want to tell you some strange things that have happened to me. But I want to think about what you have told me first," Diana said.

"I'll come over tonight. We can talk then," Mark said.

They rode back to the house. Jenny met them at the door.

"How did the riding lesson go?" Jenny asked.

"Diana rides like she was born to it," Mark said, smiling.

"He means I didn't fall off once," Diana said.

Mark took her hands. "Don't worry too
much. We will try to work it out tonight," he
said in a low voice.

The day went by slowly for Diana.

Outside, the day had turned gray and rain
had begun to fall. Diana sat by the window,
watching the rain splash against the glass.

At dinner Mr. Lang said, "Who wants to go into town tonight? A woman is giving a talk on weed control."

"In this rain?" Jenny said. "Besides, I have to finish a letter."

Mr. Lang said, "How about you, Diana?"

"I'm afraid I have to finish a letter, too," Diana said. *Now why did I say that?* she asked herself.

"Who are you writing to?" Jenny asked.

Diana started to answer but she stopped. Her head was light and her heart was beating fast. She had started to say she was writing a letter to Ian Mackenzie. A man who had been dead two hundred years.

Diana said quickly, "And Mark Woodburn is coming over."

"Maybe he would rather go to the talk instead," Mr. Lang said.

It took Diana a minute to see that he was joking.

Mark came over soon after Mr. Lang left for town in his car.

"I'll go up and finish my letter," Jenny said.

"Please stay," Diana said. "I want you to hear what I say to Mark."

CHAPTER **6**

## A LETTER TO IAN

Diana told Mark about the girl screaming in the pond. She told Jenny about the girl in the graveyard. The girl Mark had not seen. She told about the face in the mirror. And about walking in her sleep and looking for something outside.

"I don't know how to explain it," Diana said. "Maybe I am going out of my mind."

Mark said quickly, "I don't believe that. And don't *you* believe it."

"We have been friends too long for me to believe any such thing," Jenny said.

Diana said, "Why did I dream about a pond? That was before I ever found out there once had been a pond here."

"There is a pond in that picture of Elizabeth Angus. You saw the picture the first night," Jenny pointed out. "Maybe that is why you dreamed about a pond."

"That's possible," Diana said. "And maybe I didn't really see a girl in the graveyard. The sun was in my eyes. The graveyard is dark with all those tall trees. Maybe the light played a trick on my eyes."

But she didn't really believe her words. Mark could see that, too.

"But you still think it was something else, don't you?" he said. "You think it was a ghost."

"Yes," Diana said slowly. "Yes, I do."

Jenny said, "Well, I don't believe in ghosts."

"I don't either," Mark said. "And it doesn't have to be a ghost. It might just be this house. I think that some old houses hold on to their past. Past feelings, that is. A sad past can stay on. Or a happy one. That's all there is to it."

"Maybe," said Diana. "There are so many things no one knows for sure. But sometimes I have a strong feeling that there *is* someone here. Someone sad who needs help."

"What kind of help? Don't you think you could make things worse by trying to help?" Mark said. "You could get hurt. You could be playing with fire."

"Maybe," Diana said. "All I know is, I feel that someone is asking me to help."

"Diana, I want you to stop thinking about it," Mark said. "The more you think about it, the more real it will seem. So put it out of your mind. For your own good."

"Mark is right," Jenny said.

"You think I am making all of this up," Diana said in a cold voice. "You think I am going out of my mind."

Mark said, "I think you don't know if it is real or not. But I'm afraid you will talk yourself into it. We all do that kind of thing. Please don't be angry. We only want to help you."

"I know, Mark," Diana said. "And you are right . . . I will try to do what Jenny did. When I see something strange, I will tell myself it isn't happening."

And Diana really did mean to do that.

Mark left. He had to be at work early the next morning.

Diana heard herself say, "I'll go up now, Jenny. I must finish my letter." *There it was again. The letter to Ian.*

She ran up the stairs before Jenny could question her.

In her room she said, "No, I will not think about it. I will not think about Ian or letters.

Ian Mackenzie is dead. He died two hundred years ago."

She got ready for bed. She put a chair in front of her door and got into bed. But she could not lie still.

Diana walked up and down the room in the dark. She said, "I must get hold of myself. I will read for a while."

She sat in the soft chair beside the table with the oil lamp. She tried reading a book. But the book did not interest her now.

Diana got up and walked again. She stopped and looked at the big music box. Diana picked up the old box. She took it near the oil lamp to see it better.

Suddenly she almost dropped the box. The bottom was loose. The bottom piece had started to slip off.

She took off the bottom piece to see if she could fix it. Some sheets of paper spilled out.

"A hiding place!" she said. "I must have touched the right spot to open it."

The papers were stiff and hard to open. Diana was afraid she might tear them.

She was able to open one a little way. She saw the words: "When the war is over, I will stay in

this new land. As soon as I am doing well, I will come for you. In a few years it won't matter if your father is willing or not."

A few sheets of paper were not folded. Diana picked them up. She brought them close to the oil lamp.

It was a letter. "My dear Ian," it began.

A letter to Ian! Diana's hands were shaking so much it was hard to read the letter. She had to sit down.

"My dear Ian," she read again.

"So much has happened this day. The painting of me is finished at last. But, oh what trouble it caused!

"I wore the gold locket you gave me while I was sitting for the painting. I wanted it to be in the picture.

"I remember your last words before we parted. You said to wear the locket always and wait for you. Then I will know that we will meet again. When I look at your picture in it, I feel that we are together still.

"I always wore the locket next to my heart, out of sight. But I wanted the locket to show in the painting. I did not think Father would notice it. But he did.

"Today Father saw the painting for the first time. At first all he said was that the painter had done a fine job. Then Father saw the locket in the painting.

"He asked why he had never seen it before. I had to tell him that you gave it to me. He was so angry.

"He took the locket away from me. He threw it as far as he could. I saw it fall at the edge of the pond near a young tree. Father thought it had landed in the pond. He told me I would never see it or you again.

"He doesn't know he will never see me again. It is almost dark now. There is a storm. I can go out now to find the locket without being seen.

"Then I will ride away from here. My Aunt Mary will hide me. I have always been her favorite.

"When the war is over, I will join you as we planned. Now I will hide this letter so Father cannot find it while I am outside. I will finish it when I reach Aunt Mary's home."

That was all there was of the letter. Elizabeth had never finished it.

Diana listened to the sound of the rain. It was raining hard now.

"It must have been on a night like this," she said. "Poor Elizabeth. But it doesn't seem as if she wanted to kill herself. Far from it."

Diana put the pages of the letter back together. She put all the papers together. She would show them right away to Jenny. Her friend would have to believe her now.

She picked up a candle to take with her. But her hands were shaking. She dropped the candle on the pile of letters.

The papers caught on fire.

# CHAPTER 7
## THE LOCKET

Diana had to keep the house from burning. There was no time to think or plan. She opened the window. She threw the papers out in the rain. Tears ran down her face.

Diana lay down on the bed and had a long cry. At last she got up. She pushed the bottom of the music box in. It closed. She put the box away.

She lay in the dark for a long time. The storm was loud. Diana felt as stormy as the weather.

Finally she fell asleep. At once she began to dream.

She was by a tree at the edge of the pond. It was a stormy night. She felt around on the grass. In a flash of lightning she saw something shining on the ground.

She half stood up and reached over for it. The grass was wet. She slipped.

She screamed as she fell into the pond.

She felt herself sinking.

The weeds were so thick that she couldn't swim. She tried but she couldn't.

"Father," she screamed. "Help me! Help me!"

She heard a voice from the front of the house. "Where are you, child? Oh, what have you done! If only I could see in this rain!"

She felt herself being pulled under the water.

Diana woke up in bed shaking and cold. She lay in the dark with her eyes open for the rest of the night.

In the morning the sun was a welcome sight.

She got up saying, "This can't go on. Mark must help me. I can't think clearly any more."

She did not look forward to their talk. If only she had the letters to show him.

She decided not to talk to Jenny about it. Jenny was so matter of fact. Mark would understand better. She was afraid Jenny would go to her uncle. Mr. Lang might want to send her home. She couldn't let that happen.

Then she remembered the music box. She could show them the secret place. But she could not find the way to open it again.

"Could I have dreamed all that?" she asked herself. "Was it all a dream?"

Mark did not show up all morning. Diana's head hurt from not sleeping. She was cross all day. If only she could talk to Mark.

She spent most of the morning inside the house. Mr. Lang and Jenny had gone into town to buy some food. They had wanted her to come with them. But Diana had said no. She wanted to be by herself. She wanted some time to think about what was going on.

The old house was as quiet as a graveyard. But, still, from time to time Diana thought she heard a voice calling to her. Calling her name.

She went into the hall and looked at the picture of Elizabeth Angus. The girl in the picture seemed to be looking right at her. Her eyes seemed to be asking Diana for help.

"What do you want?" Diana said to the girl in the picture. "What do you want from me?"

But there was no answer.

In the late afternoon she went for a walk by herself. After a while she found herself near the graveyard. She decided to look at Elizabeth's tombstone again.

A man was already there. He was a thin old man. He looked tired but kind.

"You must be Diana," he said. "I am Parson Woodburn."

"How did you know who I am?" asked Diana.

Parson Woodburn said, "Oh, Mark has said a lot about you. Last night we talked a long time about your troubles. Mark looked so troubled when he came home that I made him sit down and talk about it."

For some reason Diana found it easy to talk to him. She told him about the letters and about her dream. She told him about the letters burning.

"What is it you are really afraid of?" the parson asked. "Do you think that all of this is just in your mind?"

Diana said, "I don't know which is worse. Is it better if it is all in my mind? Or if it is real?"

The parson shook his head. "Was there anything in the letters that you could not have dreamed?"

"I've been thinking so much about Elizabeth. I could have dreamed the letters and the music box. But it seemed very, very real," Diana said. "I have to find the answer."

"I wish I knew how to help you," the parson said. "I really do."

They stood looking at Elizabeth's tombstone. But there was no answer there.

The parson said, "You may never know the answer. But I do know one thing. You must stop getting mixed up in it right now. Or you will be hurt. Let it be."

He was doing his best to help. Diana smiled her thanks. She did not tell him that she couldn't let it be.

Then she saw Mark by the church. She called to him.

The parson said, "I will leave you two together." He left.

Diana told Mark about the letters.

Mark said, "I hoped that this business was all over. You said you would not think about it any more. That you would let it be."

"I didn't want to," Diana said. "But then I found the letters. I had to read them. Mark, if Elizabeth is still here, why would she stay? What do you think?"

"I've read books about things like this," Mark said. "Elizabeth might not understand that she is dead. She would be very mixed up. She died thinking only of that locket. That's all she can think of still. Maybe she never did think of anything besides herself and what she wanted."

"You mean she was a person who thought only of herself?" Diana said.

"We don't know what kind of person she was. If she is here, she is using you to get what she wants. She has no power to hunt for the locket herself. She needs you for that. Time would have no meaning for her. For some reason she can't make the break. She can't stop thinking of the world of the living. So she can't leave," Mark said. "That is what people who believe in ghosts would say."

"You want me to think only of myself," Diana said. "That is just as bad."

"I don't want you to get hurt," Mark said. "Let it be, Diana."

"Let it be! Let it be!" Diana said. "So it just goes on and on and never stops. And more people get hurt!"

"The people who get hurt are the people who don't let it be!" Mark shouted. "Can't you see that? You are in the middle of forces no one understands. I believe in you, Diana. But I don't want to believe in your strange dreams."

"You think I dreamed the letters then?" Diana said.

"Oh, Diana, can't you understand? If you don't stop this, Elizabeth will take complete control of your mind. It won't matter if a ghost is doing it. Or if you are doing it to yourself!" Mark said.

"Mark, why are we getting so angry?" Diana said. "There is no reason to be angry."

"Diana, don't you know how much I care about you? And I am so afraid for you. But you won't let me help you. You have to stop thinking about Elizabeth," said Mark.

"I can't, Mark," Diana said. "I can't."

Mark did not answer.

He turned and walked away. She knew by the way he walked that he was very angry.

Diana wanted to call after him. The words would not come.

Mark did not look back.

CHAPTER **8**

## THE BOG

Diana walked slowly toward the house. She reached the circle of trees and stopped.

Why not look for the locket now? There was not much hope of finding it. But she could try.

She remembered which tree she had walked to in her sleep. She found the tree. Then she got down and dug with her hands. The ground was soft. But the grass was thick.

She found a strong stick. That helped a little.

She dug and dug. All at once Diana felt something in her fingers. Something small. Something hard and round. She closed her hand around it and got up.

Suddenly she saw someone was watching her. It was Jenny.

"What are you doing?" Jenny asked, giving her a strange look.

"Nothing . . . nothing," Diana said, hiding the locket in her hand.

"You had better come in the house now," Jenny said. "It's time for dinner." Diana could see the worried look on Jenny's face. Why had Diana been digging in the ground? Jenny was afraid that her friend was going out of her mind.

During dinner Diana couldn't keep her mind on what the others were saying. They talked to her. She hardly heard them. Once in a while she caught Jenny looking at her with worried eyes.

Soon after dinner, Diana said she was going up to her room.

Mr. Lang asked, "Do you want us to call you when Mark comes?"

"He won't come tonight," Diana said.

"Of course he will," Mr. Lang said.

Jenny looked at Diana. Diana looked away.

In her room she sat down in the big chair. She closed her eyes.

One part of her mind said, "I will go to bed. I'll get a good night's sleep."

Another part said, "Wait here. Wait until it is safe to go. He is waiting for you. Your true love is waiting for you."

It was late at night when she left her room.

In her hand was the old locket. It was covered with dirt. As she walked, she rubbed off the dirt.

She opened her hand. The locket was shining in the light of the moon.

Now she was near the graveyard. "That is a place for the dead. I do not belong there. No matter what they say."

She looked all around. Where was he?

"Ian," she called. "Here I am, Ian, my love. I have the locket. Now we can be together again. Where are you?"

There he was. Ian Mackenzie. Over to the left. By the bog.

She could see him clearly by the light of the moon. Ian Mackenzie was waiting for her.

Far behind her she heard a voice. It was Jenny.

"Diana! Where are you going. Oh, dear, you are walking in your sleep again. I followed you from the house. Diana! Stop!"

The voice did not mean anything to her. The name did not mean anything to her. Who was Diana? She was Elizabeth. Elizabeth Angus.

She kept on walking toward the ghost of Ian Mackenzie. A ghost only she could see. He waited for her, smiling.

There was another voice. A man's voice, from the graveyard. It was Mark.

"Diana! Wait! I've been walking here all night. We will work things out together, Diana."

She kept on walking. Mark's voice and his words had no meaning for her.

"Diana! Don't go that way. Stop where you are!" Mark shouted. "You will sink in the bog!"

"Oh, Mark, we can't get to her in time!" said Jenny.

"Go back and get a rope. Run as fast as you can," Mark shouted. "She is walking into the bog. She will drown!"

Diana kept going. She was close to the ghost of Ian now.

"Come to me," the ghost said. "I will lead you home, Elizabeth."

She began to run to him.

Suddenly she could not move her feet. She fell forward.

She began to sink into the bog.

"Ian! Help me!" she screamed.

"Diana, can you hear me? It's Mark. I love you, Diana. I need you."

Ian held out his arms. "Come to me, Elizabeth. Come to me."

All at once she knew.

"No, Ian!" Diana screamed. "No! I can't! I'm not—" And then her mind was a blank.

Where was she? How did she get into the bog? She remembered going up to her room after dinner. She did not remember anything after that. Nothing at all.

Was this real? Or was she dreaming again?

By the light of the moon, she saw a man and a woman. They walked hand in hand over the bog. The woman was holding something in her hand—the locket. Then Diana couldn't see them any more.

"Diana! Can you hear me?"

"Mark!" she screamed. "Oh, Mark!" She was sinking fast into the bog.

"I can't reach you," Mark said. "Don't move. That will only make it worse."

"Help me, Mark! Do something! Please!" Diana said. She could feel herself being pulled down into the bog.

Mark took off his tie and his belt. He tied them together. He held one end and threw the other toward her.

She tried to grab it several times. Each time she went down deeper into the bog.

She could hardly lift her arms now. But at last she caught it.

"Hold on with both hands, Diana. It will break if I try to pull you out. But it will keep you from sinking as fast," Mark said. He kept talking to her until Jenny came running with the rope.

He tied one end of the rope to the tie and belt.

"Pull it toward you," Mark said.

Diana tied the rope under her arms. She held the rope with her hands.

Mark and Jenny pulled on it as hard as they could. Slowly they pulled Diana from the bog.

Just in time. Another minute and she would have gone under and drowned.

Mark held her in his arms. "It's going to be all right now," he said.

Diana's mind was still mixed up. "But, Mark," she said. "What about the others? We must help them."

"The others?" Mark said.

"A man and a woman. I don't know who they are. I saw them walking on the bog. Didn't you see them?" Diana said.

Mark said nothing for a minute. He looked out across the empty bog.

Then he turned and looked into Diana's eyes. "It's all right, Diana," he said. "It is done with. Elizabeth Angus and Ian Mackenzie are together again at last . . . Now it is time for us to begin, you and I."